3

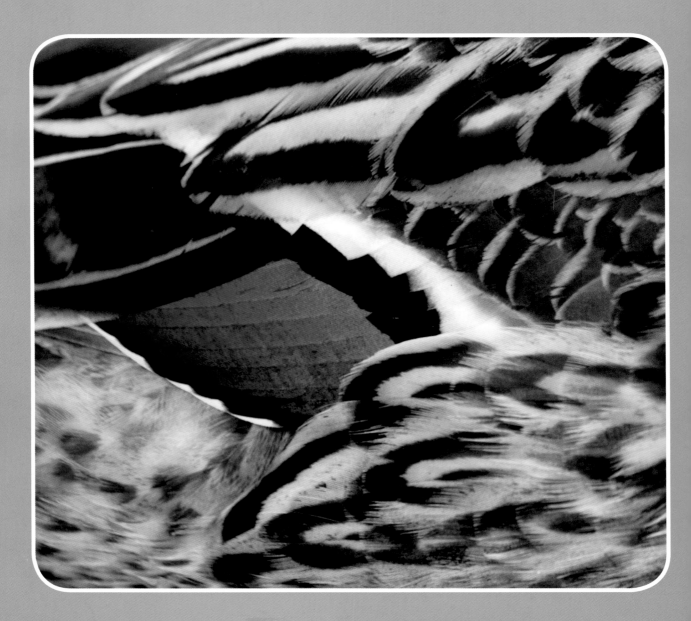

Who has a coat made of feathers?

duck

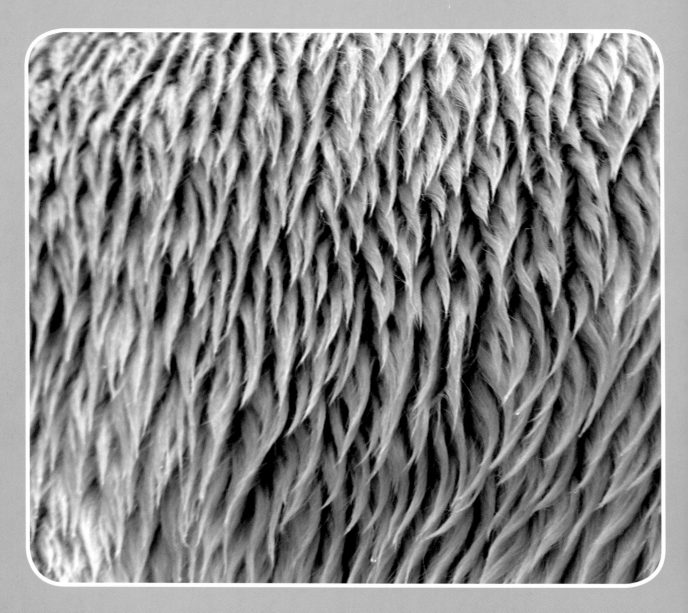

Who has a coat made of fur?

bear

Who has a coat made of shell?

tortoise

Who has a coat made of scales?

snake

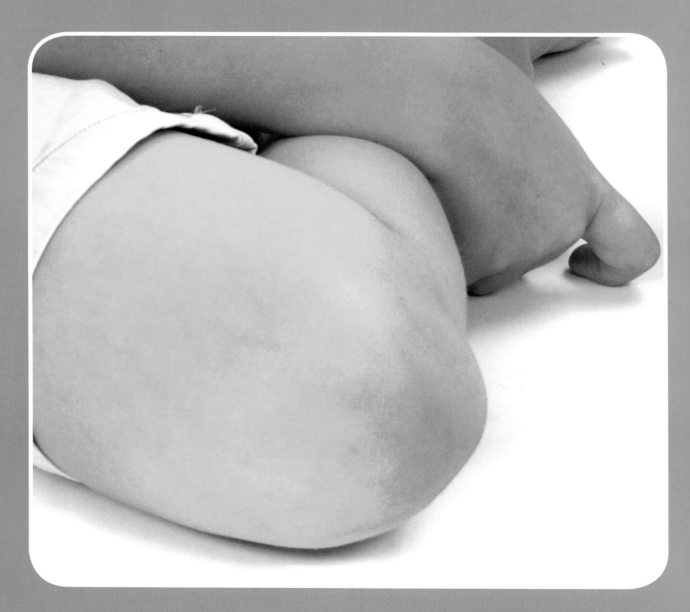

Who has a coat made of skin?

me

13

Animal coats

Ideas for reading

Written by Clare Dowdall BA(Ed), MA(Ed)
Lecturer and Primary Literacy Consultant

Learning objectives: read simple words by sounding out and blending the phonemes all through the word from left to right; read a range of familiar and common words and simple sentences independently; use talk to organise, sequence and clarify thinking, ideas, feelings and events; extend their vocabulary, exploring the meaning and sounds of new words; show an understanding of how information can be found in non-fiction texts to answer questions about where, who, why and how

Curriculum links: Knowledge and Understanding of the World: Exploration and investigation; Creative Development: Exploring media and materials

Interest words: coat(s), animal(s), who, feathers, duck, fur, bear, shell, tortoise, scales, snake, skin

High frequency words: we, all, I, a, of, me

Resources: feely bag with different materials; photographs of different animals

Word count: 44

Getting started

- Using a feely bag, invite children to feel different materials, e.g. feather, fur, leather.

- Ask children where the materials come from and what they can be used for, e.g. *to keep warm.*

- Explain that the book is about different sorts of animal coats. Read the title and blurb, pointing to each word with your finger and encouraging the children to join in.

- Look carefully at the animals in the photograph on the front cover. Ask children to identify the animals and describe their coats and what they are for.

Reading and responding

- Turn to pp2–3. Read aloud with the children, pointing to each word as you read. Model blending *c-oa-t*, and using contextual information to read the words.

- Look carefully at the pictures on pp2–3. Discuss where the children might be, what they need to wear to keep warm and dry, and why.